This book is dedicated to all who find Nature not an adversary to conquer and destroy, but a storehouse of infinite knowledge and experience linking man to all things past and present. They know conserving the natural environment is essential to our future well-being.

CRATER LAKE
THE STORY BEHIND THE SCENERY®

by Ronald G. Warfield, Lee Juillerat, Larry Smith

Ronald Warfield, a National Park Service career professional, was Chief Park Naturalist at Crater Lake for several years. Ron is a Colorado State University graduate in Forestry and Natural Resources. Lee Juillerat has written about Crater Lake for newspapers and magazines for many years. Larry Smith spent twenty years as a seasonal park ranger at Crater Lake and has collected and preserved much of the park's oral and written history.

Crater Lake National Park, located in south central Oregon, was established in 1902 to preserve this deep blue lake encircled by multicolored lava walls.

Front cover: Crater Lake, photo by David Muench. Inside front cover: Clark's nutcracker, photo by Jeff Gnass. Title page: Western pasqueflower, photo by David Muench. Pages 2/3: Crater Lake and Wizard Island, photo by Ed Cooper.

Book design by K. C. DenDooven. Edited by Peter Howorth.

Fourth Printing, 1991
CRATER LAKE: THE STORY BEHIND THE SCENERY. © 1982 KC PUBLICATIONS.
LC 82-82579. ISBN 0-916122-79-4.

Crater Lake: overwhelmingly yet sublimely beautiful. Moody. At times brilliantly blue, ominously somber; at other times buried in a mass of brooding clouds. The lake is magical, enchanting—a remnant of fiery times, a reflector of its adjacent forested slopes, a product of Nature's grand design.

A Fiery Legacy

Few places on earth command overwhelming awe from observers, but Crater lake, in south central Oregon, certainly does. Even in a region of volcanic wonders, Crater Lake can only be described in superlatives. Stories of the deep blue lake can never prepare visitors for their first breathtaking look from the brink of this huge *caldera* (a Spanish term for caldron) which is some four thousand feet deep and up to six miles wide. Even seasoned travelers gasp at the twenty-mile circle of cliffs, tinted in subtle shades and fringed with hemlock, fir, and pine: all this reflected in a lake of indescribable blue.

No one stands on the rim for long without wondering what stupendous forces created this beautiful place. Many visitors recognize that the gentle slopes outside the rim resemble the sides of other Cascade volcanoes, so it is not difficult to imagine that a similar mountain once stood here. The story of its growth and destruction is revealed in the walls of the caldera containing the lake.

Mount Mazama began the climactic eruptions that led to its collapse 6,850 years ago. Photographs of Mount St. Helens' eruption in 1980 are strikingly similar to this painting of Mount Mazama by Paul Rockwood.

COURTESY NPS

Oregon's history goes back at least two hundred million years. At that time, a huge block of the earth's crust, underlying the sea off the Pacific Northwest, began inching its way toward the continent. This heavy block of basalt lava, called the Juan de Fuca oceanic plate by geologists, was descending below the lighter continental plate.

As this oceanic plate descended beneath the continental plate, it began to melt. Magma formed from a molten mixture of the oceanic plate, the mantle material, and the continental crust. (Such magma, if erupted as lava, is called andesite, named after the Andes Mountains where such material makes up nearly all the major volcanoes.)

Long before the Cascades were formed, as the Juan de Fuca plate slid beneath the continen-

tal margin, it formed a trench extending from the southwest to the northeast across what is now Oregon. Sediments accumulated in this trench and later were transported toward the continent. Coastal mountains formed when sandstone, shale, and other sediments were scraped off the oceanic slab as it dived under Oregon. These sediments were heated and compressed to form the metamorphic rocks now exposed in the Klamath Mountains of southwest Oregon and the Blue Mountains of northeast Oregon.

About sixty million years ago, the ocean floor near the coast rose above the water, moving the shoreline westward beyond its present position. In response to these disturbances, volcanic activity began in the Pacific Northwest. Lava formed

sheets more than five thousand feet thick. At the same time, basalt poured out of undersea fractures. For millions of years, these flows accumulated in expansive sheets beneath the sea instead of forming volcanic cones. By fifty million years ago, no less than fifty thousand cubic miles of basalt had been spread upon the ocean floor. These altered lavas now form the core of the coastal ranges of Oregon.

This underwater volcanism ceased forty or fifty million years ago, but other volcanoes began to erupt on land. Andesite was predominant in the lavas that emerged. Many of these volcanoes developed into a line that became the Cascade Range, although millions of years would elapse before a continuous, high, volcanic chain formed.

The climate of Oregon was uniform at this time. Mild, humid, semi-tropical conditions pre-

ED COOPER

volumes of ash deluged eastern Oregon from these explosive eruptions.

Volcanic activity in the Pacific Northwest increased considerably fifteen to twenty million years ago. Lavas generally erupted from long fissures in the earth's surface rather than from cones. Great floods of basalt poured out over eastern Oregon and Washington, forming the almost level Columbia Plateau that covers two hundred fifty thousand square miles.

Fifteen million years ago, nearly all of Oregon was an unbroken plateau of dark basalt. Lavas and fragmental material continued to build the southern Cascades. Had the land not sagged as these lavas accumulated, the Cascades would have become high enough at the time to stop ocean winds from providing moisture to eastern Oregon.

Today, the Cascade Range is composed of two separate rows of mountains, the Western and the High Cascades. None of the original volcanic landscape is evident in the Western Cascades. The canyons and ridges are the eroded remains of volcanic accumulation some ten to sixty million years old. The High Cascades, however, are made up of younger cones that are easy to recognize even though many have been reshaped by glacial erosion.

About ten million years ago, the entire Cascade Range was elevated, folded, and tilted. In the Crater Lake region, the range was thrust upward along steeply inclined fracture planes. This uplift opened many north-south fissures along the crest of the range. For the first time, eastern Oregon was cut off from the moist sea breeze and began to grow drier.

Through fissures in the crest of the range, lavas formed a chain of large shield volcanoes in the shape of inverted saucers. Although earlier volcanoes had spewed lavas and fragments, these volcanoes oozed quiet flows of basalt. Later in their development, they became explosive and built cinder cones on their summits. A central

vailed over the entire state because the volcanoes of the Cascade Range were too low and widely spaced to form a barrier to the moist westerly winds flowing in from the Pacific.

Over the next twenty million years, the volcanoes of Oregon belched lava and showers of pyroclastic material (fire-broken fragments). The land alternately rose and subsided as the volcanoes grew larger and more numerous. Great

7

Phantom Ship appears to sail away from Sun Notch on the caldera rim. Phantom Ship is a part of the original cone which was buried by Mount Mazama. Earlier, as the mountain grew, it was carved by glaciers. A glacier once extended many miles downslope from Sun Notch. The characteristic U-shaped valley remains, cut off in cross section by Mount Mazama's collapse.

Mount Scott may be one of the largest of the overlapping volcanoes of Mount Mazama. Mazama Rock (foreground) was formed late in Mount Mazama's life. Lava flow patterns are preserved in the rock. Note the rubble on top and the vertical joints produced when lava oozed back into the caldera.

JEFF GNASS

plug of lava invaded each cone. All these shield volcanoes have been reduced by erosion to radiating ridges separated by deep canyons. The summit cones have been denuded to reveal the more resistant lava plugs standing out like miniature Matterhorns on the Cascade landscape. Union Peak, southwest of Crater Lake, and Mount Thielsen, to the north, are conspicuous examples of these old volcanoes.

The climate became much cooler about a million years ago. As winter snow accumulated in thicker packs, glaciers formed on the Cascades. The ice age descended upon North America.

The volcanoes produced during the ice age,

as well as the recent ones, had a different shape. These were composite cones resulting from diversified lava eruptions and the explosive discharge of fragments. Sometimes these volcanoes were inactive for long periods, only to begin quietly oozing andesite lava, then violently spewing out fragmental material.

Most composite cones retained their basic shape even as they were sculptured by glaciers. Some outstanding peaks of the Cascades are among these volcanoes. They grew upon the eroded remains of the old shield cones and are now aligned in a north-south belt. The present range is high enough to stop the moisture-laden

sea air from reaching the east side, which is a high desert today.

The Life and Death of Mount Mazama

Mount Mazama, the remains of which enclose Crater Lake, began to form less than seven hundred thousand years ago. It rose from a foundation of older volcanic rocks between five and six thousand feet above sea level, and probably attained an elevation of as much as twelve thousand feet. It was likely never a single cone, but rather a tight cluster of low, overlapping volcanoes. The main vent either had several smaller cones on its flanks, or the center of activity changed from time to time. Mount Scott, now the highest point in the park, may have been the largest of the cones associated with the main vent.

The oldest visible lava (about four hundred thousand years old) of Mount Mazama came from a vent close to Phantom Ship on the south wall of the present caldera. The products of this vent formed a triangular cone now exposed about a third of the way up Dutton Cliff. Fissures radiated from this area, and as the lava hardened in the cracks, it formed tough upright slabs called dikes.

The remains of one such dike form the "sails" of Phantom Ship. Lava erupted later, completely burying the Phantom cone.

From the angle of the lava on the wall of the caldera, geologists calculate that the major vent of the Mount Mazama cone was not directly above the center of Crater Lake; instead, it was almost a mile south.

As Mount Mazama rose, more lava was produced than fragmental materials, so the mountain was probably not as steep or tall as other Cascade volcanoes. The volcano grew almost entirely by the oozing of andesite lava and small ash eruptions from closely spaced vents. As it grew, its conical shape was eroded by glaciers.

In the past several hundred thousand years, at least four major glacial advances and retreats occurred. Clear evidence of glaciation can be seen at several locations on the caldera wall. The last glaciers polished, grooved, and scratched the lava surfaces of the volcano. This is evident in many places along the rim. The glaciers also carved deep, U-shaped valleys on the slopes of the volcano. Sun and Kerr notches represent the remains of two glacial valleys.

At the peak of the last ice age, about twenty-five thousand years ago, some glaciers were more than a thousand feet thick, and several extended down the mountainside as much as seventeen miles. Except for the crests of a few ridges and around the active vents, the entire mountain was clothed in a mantle of ice. As the climate gradually warmed up, these tongues of ice dwindled. Meanwhile, pumiceous ash erupted from the summit crater, while basaltic cinder cones and domes of a lava rich in silica, called dacite, formed on the lower slopes.

During Mount Mazama's growth, its sides split as the mountain bulged from the increased pressure of the magma chamber below. At least twenty of these fractures, filled with lava, are exposed as dikes on the walls. Devil's Backbone is the largest, extending from the lake shore all the way to the rim.

ED COOPER

Remnants of the pyroclastic cone atop
Mount Thielsen. Glaciers sculptured the cone,
leaving the resistant core as a horn-shaped peak.

While glaciers were advancing, then shrinking, from fifty to ten thousand years ago, a semicircular line of volcanic vents developed on the northern side of Mount Mazama, well below the summit, along what is now the northern rim of Crater Lake. Many thick flows of lava erupted from this area, among them the andesites that formed Hillman Peak and the Watchman, and the glassy dacites of Redcloud Cliff.

At about the same time this activity took place, many cinder cones of red and black basalt erupted on the lower flanks of the mountain, while several large, dome-shaped mounds of dacite formed at the eastern foot of Mount Mazama. By about eight thousand years ago, no glaciers stretched beyond the rim. Even the glaciers on the south slope in Munson, Sun, and Kerr valleys had melted.

Geologists disagree as to what was happening beneath Mount Mazama several thousand years ago. Some say that through a long calm period, the magma in the shallow feeding chamber under Mount Mazama was slowly crystalizing. The heavy crystals sank in this molten liquid while gas-charged froth rose toward the top of the chamber. If an eruption were to relieve pressure from the chamber, the gases would escape from the magma, causing lava or fragments to spew out the vent.

Other geologists maintain that basalt magma

Mount Mazama cracked from the pressure of the underground magma chamber. Lava filled at least twenty of the cracks, flowing onto the surface from vents on the northern flanks. The new lavas were resistant to erosion, so they survived as spires and dikes. Hillman Peak is the central plug of one volcanic vent exposed by Mazama's collapse. Devil's Backbone is the largest and one of the youngest dikes.

Glaciers flowed seventeen miles down the sides of Mount Mazama prior to its collapse. Striations and polish from these glaciers can be seen in many areas along the rim. This example is near North Junction on Rim Drive. Glaciers also carved the Kerr and Sun notches on the far side of the lake.

DAVID MUENCH

Llao Rock is one of the youngest and most prominent lava flows on the rim. The twelve hundred-foot-thick mass flowed over the crater from an earlier pumice eruption.

The Cleetwood lava flow erupted in the process of dome building. This flow was still hot enough when Mount Mazama collapsed that parts oozed back into the caldera, causing the lava surface to crack.

generated in the earth's mantle moves upward, melting some of the crustal rocks. This molten liquid has a composition like dacite. Blobs of liquid migrate toward the surface. If more basalt magma encounters this material, turbulent mixing occurs as heat is transferred from the basalt to the dacite. If equal parts of dacite and basalt are involved in this mixing, andesite is formed. This may explain why most of these volcanoes were built of andesite.

According to this theory, dacite magma may have established a chamber only a few miles beneath Mount Mazama. A rising blob of basalt may have encountered this volatile material, causing mixing and the escape of gases in the magma chamber. This would result in frothy magma which could erupt as a spongelike pumice if the pressure found a vent to the surface.

Whatever went on under the volcano, the stage was set for the tremendous eruptions that would destroy the top of Mount Mazama. At that time, the magma chamber had become layered with heavier basalt on the bottom, andesite in the middle, and lighter dacite on top, along with rhyolite, which was even richer in silica than dacite. The mountain's height had been reduced, possibly by explosive eruptions and by glaciation, but the summit was still above ten thousand feet.

The first murmurings of the huge eruptions that would follow occurred over seven thousand years ago on the north flank of Mount Mazama at Redcloud Cliff and Llao Rock. First, towering columns of pumiceous ash blasted through the vents. This material was carried east-southeast by the winds. Then thick lava domes grew in the new craters. Llao Rock is the remains of one twelve hundred-foot-thick flow. Later, the same process produced the Grouse Hill dome and the Cleetwood lava flow north of the main crater. The Cleetwood flow was still hot enough to ooze back down the crater wall as Mount Mazama collapsed.

Pressure on the top of the magma chamber was so reduced by the time of the Cleetwood flow that a new, violent phase of eruptions began. The reduced pressure allowed gas to explode from the magma, causing a stupendous cloud of pumiceous ash to be blown from the volcano. Southwesterly winds carried clouds of ash over hundreds of thousands of square miles of Oregon, Washington, Idaho, Nevada, Montana, Alberta, British Columbia, and Saskatchewan. More than five thousand square miles of central Oregon were buried to a depth of six inches. The volume of these falls of pumice may have reached nearly eighteen cubic miles.

The eruptions continued as the gas escaped from the frothy magma. But the last eruption was shut off almost as quickly as it had begun when the volcano began to crack and founder because the support for the roof of the magma chamber had been removed.

As the mountain started to founder, multiple vents opened up around the rim. Explosions of pumiceous ash began anew, more furiously than ever. This time ash exploded upward but parts of the cloud settled near the vent, while even more pumice boiled over the walls, hurtling down the mountainside as glowing ash flows.

These flows tended to follow the contours of the land as they raced down the slopes around the mountain: some traveled more than a hundred miles an hour down old glacial valleys. The momentum was so great that one flow rushed some forty miles down the Rogue Valley; another swept across Diamond Lake and dumped a load of pumice into the North Umpqua River valley.

North and east of the volcano, where no deep canyons confined the flows, they spread in great sheets. They traveled eastward over flat ground for twenty-five miles. Such was their force that lumps of pumice over fourteen feet in diameter were carried for twenty miles. Southward, the flows poured down the valleys at Annie and Sun creeks, filling them some three hundred feet deep with pumice. Southeastward, the flows filled Sand and Wheeler Creek canyons even deeper.

As the eruption continued, the lighter dacite pumice was exhausted, and scoria, a frothy form of andesite rich in crystals, erupted. These glowing avalanches of smoke-gray scoria covered the

Mount Mazama's eruptions swept away forests or buried them, leaving lifeless wastes of ash. Since the eruptions, forests have become reestablished around the mountain's slopes. Lack of nutrients in pumice and extreme surface temperature changes have slowed recovery in some areas.

ED COOPER

buff-colored pumice, although they didn't travel as far as the earlier flows. The Pumice Desert was created north of the present caldera, as well as a conspicuous dark layer in the canyons of Annie and Sand creeks. Finally, a veneer of ash and crystals from the explosions fell on top of the flow deposits. The great eruptions had ceased.

According to one estimate, some twenty-five cubic miles of material erupted from Mount Mazama during the series of explosions. After the eruptions, the slopes of Mount Mazama were lifeless wastes of ash and lumps of pumice. Forests which once stood in the lowlands around the mountain were swept away or buried by the flows. The great heat changed wood to charcoal. Carbon-14 dating methods were used to establish the time these trees were destroyed: this occurred about 6,850 years ago.

The flows remained quite hot long after they came to rest. All the pumice and scoria-filled can-

The pinnacles of Annie and Wheeler creeks are remnants of ash flows. As the flows filled glacial valleys, vents formed and hot gases escaped. The pinnacles are cemented pipes of these ancient fumaroles; erosion has removed the softer materials.

The caldera is half filled by Crater Lake. Wizard Island is best seen from Watchman Peak. The extreme transparency of the lake allows moss to grow in deep water near the island. The intense blue we see radiates from more than one hundred twenty feet down. Yellow streaks of pine pollen contrast with the brilliant blue

yons were obscured in smoke as hot gases seethed upward through the thick deposits. Where these gases bubbled out of cylindrical vents called fumaroles, the walls of the vents were cemented due to heat and materials that had been deposited by the vapors. Erosion has left these hardened pipes standing as pinnacles along the canyons of Annie and Sand creeks.

When the last of the ash settled, an awesome sight was revealed. The mountain had disappeared! In its place was a huge caldera up to six miles wide, four thousand feet deep, and encircled by steep walls. Enormous chunks of the former mountain and large deposits of ash covered the floor of the caldera. The collapse probably began along the northern arc of vents, engulfing the entire mountain as the eruptions proceeded.

The volcano was not exhausted after the collapse of Mount Mazama. For many centuries after its creation, the caldera floor remained hot. Moreover, several eruptions took place within the caldera. Merriam Cone, near the northern wall, was formed. Thick flows of dacite oozed out near the west central part of the caldera. A flow of andesite lava may have formed the extensive flat area, now nearly two thousand feet beneath the lake surface, south of Merriam Cone. Near the western wall of the caldera, a platform of andesite lava built up and a large cone of andesite cinders formed on top, later comprising Wizard Island when the lake formed. Many andesite flows erupted around the base of Wizard Island cone. East of this cinder cone, a dome of dacite appeared.

Soon after the collapse of Mount Mazama, ground water spilled into the caldera forming a shallow lake. Later, snow and rain brought Crater Lake to its present level. Even today, thermal springs continue to discharge heat and volcanic compounds beneath the lake, but their effects are masked by the great volume of cold lake water.

FIFTY FEET OF SNOW

Like the rest of Oregon, Crater Lake has a clearly defined winter. About seventy percent of the annual precipitation occurs from November through March, while very little falls during June, July, and August. Nearly all winter precipitation

A summer thunderstorm gathers over the lake. Most precipitation falls as snow from November through March. Winters average nearly fifty feet of snow, which lasts as late as August.

falls as snow. The annual snowfall averages nearly fifty feet, so snow accumulates in deep packs. The greatest snow depth for the state of Oregon was 252 inches, measured at park headquarters in April, 1983.

Although Crater Lake is slightly south of the Pacific Northwest storm track, it is well within range of the heavy storms that strike the coast each winter. These storms, along with the normal movement of sea air, bring a supply of moist air to Oregon.

The land becomes colder than the ocean from late fall until early spring. In winter, incoming wet air masses dump great quantities of snow as they rise along the slopes of the Cascade Range.

This situation is reversed in late spring, summer, and early fall as the land becomes considerably warmer than the ocean. Then, despite the cooling due to increased elevation, air tempera-

tures in the mountains are much higher than at the shoreline because the ground becomes so warm. Large-scale storms seldom come at this season, so very little moisture reaches the mountains. Some thunderstorms occasionally occur, but generally the weather is clear and sunny.

Precipitation varies considerably at Crater Lake National Park. The greatest variance takes place on the eastern slope. Here, the average precipitation ranges from over sixty-five inches at the crest to under twenty-five near the eastern boundary. This sharp decline stems from the movement of nearly all storms from the west. This means that the eastern portion of the park lies in the rain and snow shadow of the High Cascades.

With all the snow, visitors expect that Crater Lake must be a very cold place and that the lake must freeze solid every winter. This usually is not the case. In fact, the lake last froze in 1949. Temperatures below freezing can be experienced any time of the year, but the coldest temperatures often occur in the lower eastern part of the park, not on the high slopes or within the caldera. This peculiar phenomenon is caused by three factors: the formation of stagnant pools of cold air on the eastern Oregon plateau; the invasion of dense, cold, Arctic air from the northeast; and the warming effects of lighter marine air riding over colder air. Arctic air does not usually reach the western Cascade slopes. The Cascade Range forms a formidable climatic barrier because of its altitude.

Only snow and rain supply water to Crater Lake: no streams or rivers bring water to it, nor do they drain it. The thermal springs beneath the lake may recirculate the water in this closed ecological system. Evaporation and seepage about equals the influx of snow and rain, so the level of the lake varies less than three feet from year to year. The surface area remains at approximately twenty square miles; the depth at 1,932 feet. Even close to shore the lake is still several hundred feet deep.

Since no streams feed Crater Lake, no flushing can occur should it become contaminated. Consequently, the National Park Service must make certain that humans do not pollute the lake. Moreover, they continue to study the lake as well as to maintain the natural system supporting it.

Crater Lake has a very low concentration of dissolved minerals, and, like distilled water, has no true color. Also, an extremely low concentration of suspended particles and organic matter in the lake allows remarkable transparency. If Crater Lake held a much greater concentration of dissolved organic matter, light would not penetrate to great depths and the lake might appear green.

Although some of the light that strikes the surface reflects the lighter blue of the sky as well as the greens and browns of the rim, the remarkable blue color of the lake itself is the result of interactions of sunlight and water molecules. When light enters the water, some is absorbed, while the rest is scattered. Each color of the spectrum of light is acted upon individually. Colors with long wave lengths—reds, yellows, and oranges—are absorbed within the first few yards of the surface. At one hundred twenty feet, these colors no longer provide any illumination. The greens are absorbed a little farther down. But colors with short wave lengths are not so easily absorbed, so blue penetrates to the greatest depths.

Blue wave lengths are scattered more effectively by the water molecules. Electrons in these molecules absorb light and begin to vibrate. These vibrating electrons then reradiate the light in all directions. The resulting light is scattered from great depths, so to observers on the rim, the lake appears conspicuously blue. But even when the mystery of the color has been revealed, visitors are still amazed at the intense blueness of Crater Lake, especially at noon on a clear summer day.

SUGGESTED READING

Cranson, K. R. *Crater Lake—Gem of the Cascades, Second Edition*. Lansing, Michigan: KRC Press, 1982.

Francis, Peter. *Volcanoes*. New York: Penguin Books, 1976.

Harris, Stephen L. *Fire Mountains of the West, The Cascade and Mono Lake Volcanoes*. Missoula Montana: Mountain Press Publishing Co., 1988.

Williams, Howel. *Ancient Volcanoes of Oregon*. Eugene, Oregon: University of Oregon, 1962.

Williams, Howel. *Geology of Crater Lake National Park, Oregon*. Washington, D.C.: Carnegie Institution, 1942.

RAY ATKESON

Visitors expect that the lake will freeze every winter. Actually, it seldom freezes because it lies above the cold Arctic air. The lake's volume allows the heat to dissipate slowly throughout the winter.

The massive eruption cloud of Mount Saint Helens on May 18, 1980, was impressive to the people in Washington State. About three-tenths of a cubic kilometer of magma erupted into the atmosphere. The earlier eruptions of Mount Mazama probably appeared similar to Native Americans then living in eastern Oregon. The ash cloud in Mazama's final eruptions, however, reached fifty-some cubic kilometers of ejected magma. The resultant ash fall covered two hundred fifty thousand square miles and extended as far as Saskatchewan. The flows of ash traveled only a short distance from Mount Saint Helens, but the ash flows boiled out of Mazama, rushing thirty-five miles down the Rogue River valley, covering Klamath Marsh twenty-five miles away, and spreading eastward in great sheets for twenty-five miles. The flows carried pumice blocks fourteen feet in diameter to Chemult, twenty miles from the volcano.

Mount Saint Helens developed within the last twenty-five hundred years. Mazama was a much older structure before its collapse.

Mt. St. Helens
May 18, 1980

Mount Saint Helens was the most perfect composite cone in the High Cascades before its eruption, but Mount Mazama was probably a cluster of overlapping volcanoes with a much less imposing profile.

Mount Saint Helens' stature was much reduced by its eruption, triggered by failure of the north flank, which caused a tremendous landslide. The blast was partially directed northeast, devastating 150 square miles. Already, a new dome is forming in the crater as the mountain rebuilds itself.

RAY ATKESON

RAY ATKESON

The Forested Slopes

All approaches to Crater Lake's caldera meander through different types of forests. The distribution of conifers in these forests is influenced by their environmental tolerances, which places them into a mosaic pattern of habitats. Thus, forests of Ponderosa pines and white firs thriving near the south entrance area contrast vividly with dwarf forests of whitebark pine blanketing the slopes of Cloudcap and Mount Scott.

The primary environmental feature of the lower forest is the longer growing season. It is especially warm and dry there compared to the highest whitebark pine woodland, where it is like winter much of the year and the growing season is short.

Natural fires are an essential element in maintaining the lower forests. Fires have had a significant role in perpetuating certain plants as well as communities of plants. Although all the natural fires were suppressed in the past, new policies aim to restore the natural role of fire in these forests. Current research on this role will provide essential information on how to manage nature's processes within old-growth forests.

The forest mosaic of the park includes dense stands of lodgepole pines occupying pumice flats. These flats are especially hostile, for frequent frosts occur during the growth season, and the soil is low in nutrients. The forests are very susceptible to mountain pine beetle outbreaks, insect infestations which may occur when the stands are eighty to a hundred years old.

Historic outbreaks of such insects have turned large forests of lodgepole pines into seas of silvered, weathered snags. Such a scene was typical in the late 1920s, when many areas beyond the north rim were infested. Lodgepole pines are very well adapted to natural forces, however, and are highly resilient following disturbances from

LLOYD SMITH

Through eighty years of aggressive fire control, ground fuels built up and white fir invaded the ponderosa pine forests. Fires once perpetuated many species of trees. Several years ago, however, the National Park Service did some controlled burns to restore this natural balance and help preserve the ponderosas.

Whitebark pines, distorted by severe environmental conditions, live on Mount Scott and along the northern rim.

Staghorn lichen clings to the branches and bark of slow-growing trees throughout the park.

Shasta red fir is found at middle and upper elevations. Some fine stands are near the park headquarters, while others occur among the hemlocks near Rim Village. Their stiff branches and open crowns allow them to withstand heavy snow loads. Unique snowflake patterns of branches; reddish, furrowed bark; and cones that grow upright on the upper branches identify this tree from a distance.

both insects and fires. Moreover, they are prolific seed producers.

In addition to the pumice flats, pumice fields lie within the park, but they support little tree life and only several hardy herbaceous species. The most prominent pumice field, called the Pumice Desert, lies along the north entrance road. Moisture does not limit plant growth here; instead, low levels of vital nutrients and hostile surface temperature changes make this an unfavorable environment.

Contrasting with these sites are moist meadows fringed with tall subalpine firs. These spire-shaped trees have short branches that do not break easily under heavy loads of snow.

Many shaded slopes are forested with old growth mountain hemlocks. These trees depend on deep snow packs to insulate the soil from very cold temperatures and to provide essential moisture during the winter dormant period. The deep shade beneath these stands allows little under-growth except for the smooth woodrush, which is highly dependent upon low, filtered light.

The most common true fir of the high slopes is the Shasta red fir. It is especially prominent along the eastern Cascade crest. It grows best in open, sunny locations. Its cones, like all true fir cones, grow upward from the higher tree limbs. Once mature, the cones disintegrate, dispersing many winged seeds. Because of their prolific seed dispersal method, Shasta red firs often invade burned sections of land. But many were burned themselves during a lightning fire in August 1978 on the southeastern flank of Crater Peak. Lines of burned trees can still be seen at places along the road beyond Annie Creek Canyon, toward the south entrance.

The most remarkable story of Crater Lake's forests involves their comeback following Mount Mazama's climactic eruptions. All the plant and animal life was quickly erased from the landscape by this eruption. Whitebark pines must have

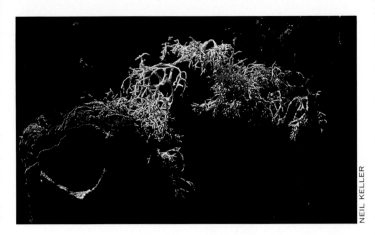

been among the first to return, for their seeds are spread by Clark's nutcrackers. These crow-like birds search diligently for seeds, descending upon the whitebark pines during autumn and prying out vast numbers of seeds for food. Some are eaten right away, but many others are cached in various spots, which oddly enough, ensures the germination and growth of seedling white-bark pines.

Lodgepole pine was undoubtedly another early invader on the barren slopes. Other plant seeds were unwittingly carried by animals or dispersed by the wind from areas beyond the zone of devastation.

Mount Mazama's eruption occurred when the climate was warm and dry, so Klamath Lake was much lower than it is today. This dry climate must have favored the expansion of the Ponderosa pine forest all the way to the rim. All of Crater Lake's vegetation, in fact, has developed over the seven thousand years since the eruption.

Stonecrop adds color to Crater Lake's gardens.

Sturdy mountain hemlocks, abundant in the park, have very flexible branches which bend easily under heavy snow loads. Staghorn lichens cannot grow below the average snow depth in this area.

Overleaf: Heavy snow creates harsh conditions avoided by most animals, but humans often enjoy the challenge.
RON WARFIELD

Rabbitbrush lends color before winter snow returns.

Purple lupine and white American bistort fill summer meadows.

Fawn lilies bloom immediately after the snow melts

Lewis monkey flower dominates Castle Crest Wildflower Trail.

A Ring of Flowers

Natural cycles greatly influence seasonal displays of flowers. Many varieties of wildflowers lie dormant ten months a year, but in just two months, they turn from seed to flower and back to seed, providing an ever-changing mosaic of colors.

The annual growth cycle begins as winter snows melt, running down the caldera walls, through the hemlock, and into the pine forests farther down. Glacier lilies burst through the thinning snowbanks on open slopes near the rim. Even before their leaves mature, the white blossoms are fluttering in the cool breezes. The waxy, white flowers of western pasque also emerge near retreating snowbanks. By midsummer they are transformed into the hoary, bearded "old men of the mountain."

Late in the spring, bright red stems of Newberry knotweed shoot up. Within a week, the inconspicuous green flowers emerge, but before summer's end, the fleshy, dull green leaves turn scarlet, then quickly wither and blow away.

Kaleidoscopes of colors and shapes blossom as the snow line retreats. Whites, purples, and lavenders glow from lupines, while penstemon, phlox, pussy paws, monkey flowers, Jacob's ladders, forget-me-nots, bleeding hearts, and others produce a paint pot of sometimes lavish, sometimes subtle hues.

The floral display is most dramatic as enclaves of flowers blossom along moist cliffs, bogs, and meadows. The most colorful pageant occurs at Castle Crest Wildflower trail, where many varieties of flowers make their seasonal appearances.

But wildflowers are more than just beautiful plants. They furnish food and protection for birds

CONNIE TOOPS

Western pasqueflower blooms near Mount Scott.

Autumn comes early to high meadows as foxtail barley puts on seed heads and groundsel adds a touch of yellow.

LLOYD SMITH

False hellebore, also known as corn lily, is abundant in moist areas.

JEFF GNASS

K. C. DENDOOVEN

The stripes on the golden-mantled ground squirrel stop at its shoulder, while the similar chipmunk has stripes over its eye.

Mule deer favor the drier eastern side of the park.

LLOYD SMITH

and animals. Their roots prevent soil from being washed away by melting snow or rainfall. When they die, they add humus to the earth, enriching it and forming a protective cover over the harsh mineral soil.

PARK WILDLIFE

Like many of the park's attractions, most forms of wildlife are seldom seen. In fact, many visitors think the wildlife is restricted to the golden-mantled ground squirrels and chipmunks that scamper about.

The largest animal, though one of the least viewed, is the elk. A herd of about 150 bases itself near Union Peak during the summer grazing in the meadows on the south side of the park. Elk are most common in open areas near timber stands, where they graze on green grasses and various shrubs. They stand up to five feet high at the shoulder and weigh up to six hundred pounds. Despite their bulk, elk have an uncanny ability to move quietly and avoid detection.

The black bear is another large resident. Panhandling bears were frequently seen in the past, but today, most bears have returned to their natural habits. Management policies have discouraged the bears' dependence on humans for food. Some bears still raid garbage cans and ice chests during the summer at Mazama Campground, however.

Taming bears and other animals is undesirable because it creates an environment where wildlife becomes a sideshow. Even worse, when animals depend on humans for food, they lose their independence. Once the seasonal visitors depart, the animals suffer because they are no longer accustomed to foraging for themselves. Although bears occasionally create problems in populated park areas, most are wary and seldom are even glimpsed by backcountry visitors.

Black bears, which actually vary from brown to black, feed on plants, small mammals, and wild berries. They are not true hibernators. Black bears maintain a body temperature near the summer norm rather than regulating it to the temperature of their winter surroundings. The winter sleep, or dormancy, of bears is an adaptation to a seasonal shortage of food and the cold weather. Black bears den under rocks, fallen trees, or other natural shelters during the cold months.

Mule and blacktailed deer can be seen fairly often. Mule deer favor the drier east side, while the smaller blacktailed deer are found in the moist meadows of the west.

Black bears are not often seen. They feed on plants, berries, or small mammals in the backcountry and are not encouraged to eat handouts.

Coyotes and bobcats are common, although they are rarely seen. Pronghorns occasionally visit the park. Other woodland residents, like skunks and porcupines, are seldom observed because they are nocturnal.

Red foxes, which actually have several color forms, are sometimes seen near Munson Valley in winter. The foxes feed on rodents, small mammals, fruits, and berries.

Yellow-bellied marmots, a favorite food of foxes, live under loose rocks. Their shrill, whistling calls often pierce the air during summer. Marmots, related to woodchucks, hibernate during winter, dropping their body temperatures and slowing their heartbeat and breathing.

Rabbitlike pikas, among the few animals that are active during the winter, are less conspicuous. Signs of their presence include small mounds of sun-dried hay along rocky talus slopes. Pikas forage for flowering plants and shrubs during the summer, which they store away in burrows for their winter food supply. Pikas are common at Garfield Peak and in rocky areas near Sun and Kerr notches.

Yellow-bellied marmots hibernate in the winter, but unlike the black bear, drop their body temperature and slow their heartbeat. Watch for marmots and rabbitlike pikas along rocky talus slopes, especially near Garfield Peak.

Red foxes, often seen in their more common dark color phase, feed on rodents.

Clark's nutcrackers pry seeds from tightly closed whitebark pinecones near the rim. Some seeds are eaten, and others cached. These hidden seeds ensure the regeneration of the pines which provide the birds with their favorite food. Every visitor to Crater Lake hears their raucous calls announcing their presence.

A Bird Watcher's Paradise

The bold and noisy Clark's nutcracker makes its presence known to virtually everyone who visits a lake overlook any time of the year. The nutcracker pries conifer seeds loose with its long, pointed bill and catches insects, usually in flight.

Ravens are often seen soaring above the rim, performing a variety of aerial antics. These birds emit a variety of croaks, squawks, and warbles. They feed on rodents, insects, worms, frogs, snakes, young rabbits, and bird eggs. Gray and Steller's jays are other notable scavengers. They steal food from visitors and collect whatever natural food is available.

The seldom-seen great horned owls, nocturnal birds, are actually common residents of the park's hemlock forests. They are the largest of the North American eared owls. Dippers, also called water ouzels, feed on a variety of water insects and their larvae. Despite the cold winters, the well-insulated dippers forage year-round on park streams and along the lake shore.

Hairy woodpeckers are a major force in controlling insects. Small brown creepers, red-breasted nuthatches, mountain chickadees, and golden-crowned kinglets also enjoy snapping up

Gray jays scavenge whatever natural foods are available. Even in winter, they can be seen near Rim Village.

A young screech owl peers from its nest.

A startling biological aspect of the lake is the presence of green moss as deep as four hundred twenty-five feet. Near Wizard Island, these mosses form a thick mat over the lake bottom some sixty to two hundred feet down. The growth of green plants this deep is quite unusual for fresh water. Such growth provides evidence of the exceptionally deep penetration of sunlight into the clear water of Crater Lake.

SUGGESTED READING

FOLLETT, DICK. *Birds of Crater Lake National Park.* Crater Lake, Oregon: Crater Lake Natural History Association, 1979.

ROSS, CHARLES R. *Trees to Know in Oregon.* Corvallis, Oregon: Oregon State University Press, 1989.

STEWART, CHARLES. *Wildflowers of the Olympics and Cascades.* Port Angeles, Washington: Nature Education Enterprises, 1988.

tree insects and spiders, whereas gray-crowned rosy finches feed on both insects and seeds. Red crossbills and dark-eyed juncos (formerly called Oregon juncos), the park's most prolific breeding birds, feed primarily on seeds.

Bird populations swell during late summer and early fall. Hikers resting atop Mount Scott are frequently treated to views of red-tailed hawks, harriers, goshawks, and golden eagles riding the thermal breezes. Bald eagles are sometimes seen along the rim searching for fish, carrion, or crippled waterfowl.

Energetic rufous hummingbirds are attracted by the varieties of summer wildflowers, while other seasonal inhabitants, like yellow-bellied sapsuckers, collect tree sap. Flickers, mountain bluebirds, pileated woodpeckers, and western tanagers feed on tree insects. Western and olive-sided flycatchers, Townsend's solitares, and yellow-rumped and Wilson's warblers rely on flies to satisfy their diets.

Other seasonal birds, such as ruffed grouse, horned larks, robins, Swainson's thrushes, evening grosbeaks, Cassin's finches, pine siskins, and various sparrows feed on the ground in search of insects, fruits, berries, and conifer seeds. Although over two hundred species of birds have been recorded in the park, many are only brief visitors during migrations.

LIFE IN THE LAKE

Fish were introduced to the lake in 1888 by William G. Steel, credited with helping to establish the park. Stocking continued until 1942. Today, rainbow trout and Kokanee salmon still thrive in the lake, feeding on water fleas, midges, and insects. In turn, the fish are a primary food source for most birds inhabiting the caldera.

Fish were introduced into Crater Lake in 1888. Fishermen occasionally catch rainbow trout near Wizard Island. Kokanee salmon also are caught.

Those Who Came Before . . .

Ancient hunters and gatherers began to inhabit southern Oregon perhaps twelve thousand years ago. The land provided ancient people with food, drink, and shelters in caves, cliffs, and forests. Early wanderers adapted to the extremes of nature but they lived in the shadow of a mountain that would soon destroy itself. We know from their legends that the Indians witnessed the final eruptions of Mount Mazama. They may not have seen the actual collapse, but they certainly felt it.

The Cascade Mountains and the surrounding spring-fed basins shaped the peoples' lives, customs, villages, and religion. During good years, the land teemed with waterfowl and plants. But the land could also be harsh with drought and cold. Even worse, billowing clouds of volcanic pumice sometimes covered thousands of square miles, requiring many years for the forests, wildlife, and fish to recover.

Seventy miles northeast of Crater Lake lies a region of dry lake beds. In the cliffs lining the old beaches are numerous caves ancient man once used for shelter. In 1938, a University of Oregon team, excavating in this region, discovered seventy-five sandals beneath an accumulation of centuries of pumice, dust, and ash. Each sandal was charred by fire from pumice which had fallen on the Indian settlement. Caked mud, burned red by the intense heat, was found between the twisted rope soles of the sandals, which were over nine thousand years old. This site, called Fort Rock today, was one of several areas where Indians lived within sight and sound of Mount Mazama.

Wizard Island looms through the early morning fog. This beautiful scene probably was not shared by Native Americans with early settlers because the Indians considered the lake a place of reverence.

DAVID MUENCH

The upper Klamath Marsh area, fifty miles southeast of Mazama, was inhabited by the Modocs for nearly twelve thousand years. (No other region in North America has been continuously occupied longer than this.) Also, three other Indian sites near Mount Mazama have been found in northern California.

Early people were drawn to regions where gathering food was easy. Marshland, fed by springs, provided a favorable habitat for birds and animals near the Crater Lake region. Bogs created a natural trap for ambushing large animals. The Indians set their dogs on the prey, then dispatched it with their stone-tipped weapons.

Such aggressive hunting methods may have caused the extinction of mastodons, ground sloths, and ancient camels. Nevertheless, these people didn't leave the marshes when hunting became more difficult. Instead, they adapted their methods for hunting the antelope, bison, mule deer, and bighorn sheep that began to inhabit the region.

But spears, string bolas, and rocks limited the types of prey the Indians could obtain. The advent of the bow and arrow revolutionized their hunting capabilities, however, and soon squirrels and small carnivorous animals, as well as an occasional elk, bear, or buffalo, supplemented their game.

Moreover, the Indians could gather food from the sky in the spring and fall as millions of migratory birds passed. Recent archaeological excavations south of Klamath Lake suggest that Native Americans had been eating waterfowl for over eight thousand years. Feathers gathered from the birds were used for arrow guides and decorations, and woven into warm blankets and body coverings.

The Indians supplemented this high protein diet with plant foods gathered from the shallow lakes and ground into flour on milling stones. Camas, Ipo tuber, wocus, and arrowleaf root provided much-needed starch. Milled grains and seeds, as well as dried fish and meat, helped the tribes survive the fierce and frozen winters.

The water tule was the most useful plant. Although it was edible, it was low in food value. It was prized for its durable fibers, however, which could be woven into baskets, mats, clothing, summer house coverings, and raftlike boats.

Even gathering plants along the shores of lakes was not always fruitful, for the waterlines of such lakes sometimes changed with little warning, disrupting the plant life and forcing the Indians to move the village sites. The water

level of these lakes was controlled by rock faults east of the Cascades which served as dams. When eruptions at Mount Mazama disturbed these dams, the water level of the lakes would fluctuate accordingly.

As people and environments changed, the Modocs became known as the Waterfowl People, because they settled near lakes and marshes that formed an ideal waterfowl habitat. Although rainfall was meager, the surrounding volcanic ridges held great quantities of water which supplied the lakes the birds favored. Abundant sunshine promoted the growth of numerous species of algae and water plants for the wildlife.

Even though this region may have been abandoned from time to time after destructive geological events, the people kept returning. As

Wood ducks were included in the diet of the Klamath Indians living south of Mount Mazama.

STEPHEN J. KRASEMANN—DRK PHOTO

Native elk (today known as Roosevelt elk) were nearly hunted out of existence in the southern Cascades by the early 1900s. In 1917, 15 Rocky Mountain elk were brought into the area to replenish the herds. The current herd of about 150 descends from the two groups.

hostile as this environment could be, it was still good to them most of the time. The collapse of Mount Mazama must have been a terrifying experience to those living so close, however. The medicine men must have been quite busy trying to appease the gods of the mountain. Probably few inhabitants were actually buried by the ash fall, but no doubt many people fled the region when the eruptions occurred, leaving behind their rich lands and hard-earned possessions.

Most Indian legends from this region deal with the powerful religious significance of how the gods controlled the eruptions. These stories not only reveal the attempts of the Indians to appease the gods, but also explain the destruction that was raining down upon them.

Vidae Falls punctuates the forest near the Rim Drive, only a few miles from park headquarters.

JOSEF MUENCH

WAYNE LANKINEN/DRK PHOTO

Scarlet paintbrush brightens sunny slopes.

CONNIE TOOPS

Several tales were told of the battles between two gods, the Chief of the Below World, *Llao,* and the Chief of the Upper World, *Skell:*

> Long ago, the spirits of the mountains often came and talked with the people. Sometimes the Chief of the Below World would come up from his home inside the earth and stand on top of the high mountain that used to be. At that time, no lake was up there.
>
> One time, while the Chief of the Below World was on earth, he saw *Loha,* the beautiful daughter of the tribal chief. The Chief of the Below World told her of his love and asked her to return with him to his lodge inside the mountain and thus attain eternal life. The maiden refused and hid herself. The Chief of the Below World became very angry. In a voice like thunder, he swore that he would destroy the people of Loha with the Curse of Fire.
>
> As he rushed through the opening and stood upon the mountain, the mighty form of the Chief of the Above World was seen descending from the sky to the top of Mount Shasta. From their mountain tops, the two spirit chiefs began a furious battle. Mountains shook and crumbled. Red hot rocks as large as hills were hurled through the skies. An ocean of fire spewed out, devouring the forests, with the flames sweeping on until they reached the homes of the People.
>
> Fleeing in terror before it, the People found refuge in the waters of Klamath Lake. As the men prayed to the Chief of the Above World for safety, they realized only a living sacrifice would turn away the wrath of fire. Two medicine men, the oldest and most revered, rose from the water and started toward the mountain of the Chief of the Below World. When they reached the top, they jumped in the pit of fire. The Chief of the Above World saw this brave act and drove the Chief of the Below World back to his home.
>
> When the morning sun rose, the high mountain was gone. The Chief of the Above World quartered the fallen chief and cast the head into the fire pit. Today it lies where it fell and strangers call it Wizard Island.
>
> The stones within the chasm soon ceased their groanings when the Chief of the Below World's body was destroyed. The fires died in great clouds of smoke. All became dark and still. The bereaved people gathered around the edge of the silent abyss and shed their tears for the fate of their chief. Their tears fell within the dark pit. Today the tears shine as clear and silent as the day they fell. We know those tears as Crater Lake.

As the volcanic activity ceased and Nature healed the scars of the eruptions, the people returned. But their way of life was soon to be destroyed by events beyond their control, something the mountain and its gods had failed to do.

LLOYD SMITH

The Lake That Never Was

Frightful tales of the recent mountain battles, repeated generation after generation, kept most Indians away from the Upper Cascades, out of sight of Mazama's new lake. Indian reverence for the area kept it undiscovered for fifty years following the white man's first exploration into the Northwest.

Lewis and Clark, who traveled across northern Oregon in 1805, alerted explorers and fur traders to the potential riches of Oregon. Because of the remoteness of southern Oregon and the lack of fur-bearing animals, the Klamath and Modoc Indians were spared contact with early mountain men for another twenty years.

Peter Skene Ogden, a fur trapper, wrote the first account of a Klamath Indian settlement when he and his men discovered twenty tent-houses in Klamath Marsh in 1829. Ogden was impressed with the ingenuity the Indians had shown in building their tent-houses over the water, which made a land attack by their neighboring enemies

Lightning and thunder disturb the stillness of Crater Lake, recalling the legendary battle between Llao and Skell.

virtually impossible. Ogden later wrote that the Indians seemed happy to see the white men. At the same time, however, they regretted that the first contact had been made.

Captain O. C. Applegate, an early pioneer, trailblazer, and Indian agent, remembered his contacts with the Indians, saying that they were ". . . of unusual energy and intelligence. The Klamaths call themselves *Ouxkane,* 'People of the Klamath Marsh,' and they have no tradition suggesting their immigration from any other country, but they claim direct descent from the followers of the Great Spirit, *Kamoo-lumps,* away back in the days when according to their mythology, he managed in person mundane affairs and the animals and birds were his intelligent subjects."

The valleys of central Oregon, including the Klamath Basin, 'soon became a major route for travelers. Groups of mountain men, trappers, explorers, and traders began to travel between the rapidly expanding empire of the Hudson Bay Company, headquartered on the Columbia River,

and the productive ranches and seaports of northern California.

General John C. Frémont and his guide Kit Carson led several scientific and reconnaissance groups through the Klamath Basin between the winter of 1843 and the spring of 1846. Frémont and his parties passed within sight of the rim of Crater Lake and the eastern slope of Mount Scott. In his journal, the general refers to a story about the "great sunken hole," although Frémont probably never actually saw Crater Lake.

A dispute with a band of Klamath Indians flared into a fight on May 6, 1846, leaving three of Frémont's men dead. In retaliation, Frémont and his party circled the north end of Klamath Lake and killed fourteen warriors. Skirmishes with the Klamaths and the more aggressive Modocs continued for the next thirty years as wagon trains of settlers headed for the rich lands of the Willamette and Rogue valleys. This trouble with the Indians continued until after the Reservation Revolt and Modoc Indian War of 1872. The rebelling

*Early discoverers of the lake called it
Deep Blue Lake or simply Blue Lake.*

Modocs were defeated the following year, their war chiefs executed, and the remaining members of the tribe shipped by train to the Oklahoma Indian Territory. This war spelled the end of the twelve thousand-year-old civilization. The Klamaths lived peacefully on the reservation bordering Crater Lake National Park until the property was sold to the U. S. Forest Service in 1959.

The discovery of gold in California started a huge migration of people in 1849. A gold strike three years later in Daisy Creek, on the western edge of the Rogue River Valley, eighty miles west of Crater Lake, brought a large influx of these miners into the new town of Jacksonville, Oregon.

In the spring of 1853, eleven California miners from Yreka stopped in for supplies at Isaac Skeeters' mercantile store in Jacksonville. Slightly drunk, one of them began to brag how he and his friends knew of certain landmarks that would direct them to the "Lost Cabin Gold Mine," where nuggets lay around like rocks. If these landmarks could be located, they would all be rich!

Overhearing the boasting, Skeeters immediately hunted up twenty-one-year-old John Wesley Hillman, recently in from the gold fields of northern California, and asked him to finance an expedition of eleven Oregonians to also search for the mine. The Hillman-Skeeters party followed at a discreet distance as the Californians headed out the next morning. The miners soon discovered the Oregonians on their trail. As rations on both

sides began to dwindle, Hillman approached the other camp, proposing that since they were both lost and looking for the same thing, they should join forces. A truce was declared and both groups began to search together.

When the provisions finally ran out, the prospectors found themselves at the headwaters of the Rogue River. Seven of them rode ahead seeking game for food.

On June 12, 1853, John Wesley Hillman, Henry Klippel, and Isaac Skeeters were riding up a long, sloping mountain when the group suddenly saw a large body of water spread out below them. Hillman exclaimed that the blue was the bluest he had seen, so Skeeters suggested that they name it Deep Blue Lake. They wrote the name on a piece of notebook paper, along with their names, and placed the note on a stick.

The following day, the prospectors encountered a party of Indians who denied any knowledge of the lake's existence. Hillman later learned from a medicine man that the lake was sacred and death would come to any Indian who gazed upon it.

Starvation soon drove the miners down the mountain and back to Jacksonville. They reported the discovery of the lake, but since gold and Indians were uppermost in the minds of the settlers, their discovery was soon forgotten.

Ten years passed before the lake was seen again, this time by Chauncey Nye and several others, who were headed toward Jacksonville from the gold fields of eastern Oregon. "The waters were of a deeply blue color, causing us to name it Blue Lake," wrote Nye in a short article in Jacksonville's *Oregon Sentinel*. This was the first description of the lake ever published.

As settlement increased in southern Oregon, so did the threat of Indian attacks. In 1863, the army established Fort Klamath seven miles east of the present park boundary. On August 1, 1865, two army hunters, John M. Corbell and F. M. Smith, spotted the lake while hunting wild game for food. Acting upon this latest discovery, a group of soldiers and several curious civilians journeyed to the lake from the fort.

Upon seeing the lake for the first time, Sergeant Stearns' enthusiasm overcame his grammar:

*Once sacred to Indians, Crater Lake draws travelers
searching for the ultimate lake. Few would argue
that this lake is the bluest, but many visitors miss views
like this along the east rim.*

Quiet moods of Crater Lake are captured as the Watchman (left) and Hillman Peak (right) loom above Wizard Island.

"That's the sky we're lookin' at. How we got so far above it?" He then climbed over the edge of the rim and became the first man to reach the shore of Crater Lake. Several others soon joined him, including Captain F. B. Sprague, who suggested the name "Lake Majesty." This appeared in print in Jacksonville two weeks later, and Lake Majesty became the name of the lake.

During July of 1869, Jim Sutton, a newspaper editor, David Linn, a cabinet maker, their families, and several friends headed out from Jacksonville to spend several days at Lake Majesty. Traveling over the rough roads in their heavily loaded wagons was dangerous and difficult. Camping two miles from the lake's rim, the men backpacked in lumber for a boat. It was soon completed and lowered over the edge.

In August, several men reached Wizard Is-

land by paddling and bailing energetically. They spent several hours climbing the cinder cone and firing their guns. Sutton wrote an article describing their trip for the Jacksonville newspaper, using the name Crater Lake for the first time. The great lake had a permanent name.

Peter Britt, Jacksonville's pioneer portrait photographer, managed to drive his photographic wagon within camera-carrying distance of the rim. He took the first photo of the lake in 1874. Britt made stereoview cards from his picture and the image was reproduced in a number of magazines. The fame of Crater Lake began to spread across the country.

THE GUARDIAN OF CRATER LAKE

Few Americans can claim to be the father of a national park. Rare is the individual who recognizes an opportunity for preservation, acts upon it, and is willing to devote a lifetime to seeing a park established.

John Muir (Yosemite), George Dorr (Acadia), and William Gladstone Steel (Crater Lake), were among the few who were able to convince Congress of the benefits of their particular park.

Steel's preoccupation with Crater Lake began in 1870, when he was a sixteen-year-old schoolboy in Kansas. One noon early in the spring, Steel sat in the window of the schoolroom eating his lunch and reading articles from the newspaper wrapped about his sandwich. A small filler article about an unusual lake in Oregon caught his attention. Little did he realize the impact that small article would have on his life and on Oregon.

The story described a special mountain lake fifteen miles in diameter, surrounded by perpendicular walls of lava five thousand feet high, with an island in the center, and containing an extinct volcano. Steel read and reread the item and resolved that some day he would find that lake and cross to the island where he would eat lunch. He talked of his idea for days.

Two years later, the Steels moved to Portland, Oregon, where young Will redoubled his efforts to find the location of Crater Lake. Seven years later, he met a man from Ashland who had visited the lake and described the wonders he had seen. In August of 1885, Steel and John Breck, a druggist from Portland, joined a group headed for Crater Lake via Fort Klamath. There they met Captain Clarence E. Dutton, also en route to the lake. Steel and Breck, anxious to reach the lake, left the main body of travelers and hurried on ahead.

William Gladstone Steel is credited with devoting his life and fortune to the establishment and preservation of Crater Lake National Park.

When the two men finally spotted the lake, the water was so blue it startled them. They both stood speechless for several minutes. Then, overcome with the spectacle before them, they sat down on the rim. At last Steel broke the silence. "Johnny, there isn't a claim around or near the lake. It all belongs to the government and it's up to you and me to save this lake."

"You are right," Breck replied, "but how are we going to do it?"

After some moments of silence, Steel answered that it should be a national park. Steel became so agitated by the idea that he became distressed. Thus began Steel's forty-nine years of involvement with Crater Lake.

Peter Britt, a pioneer photographer from Jacksonville, Oregon, took the earliest known photograph of Crater Lake in 1874.

Phantom Ship, the remains of a dike in the oldest part of the caldera wall, appears to float on Crater Lake. Best views of the Phantom Ship are from Sun or Kerr notches on the East Rim Drive.

JEFF GNASS

When Captain Dutton arrived on the rim, they spent many hours discussing the national park idea as well as the lake's mystery and inspiring beauty. The captain suggested that they circulate a petition asking President Cleveland to set aside ten townships as a public park.

To learn more about the lake, they launched a small, leaky, canvas boat and explored the shoreline and the island. Steel named several of the lake's prominent features, including Wizard Island, "because of its weird appearance," and Llao Rock, based on the old Indian legend.

On Dutton's suggestion, Steel did circulate the petitions during the fall of 1885. These documents, with prominent signatures, were presented to the President by Steel. This show of public support, plus Steel's presentation, convinced President Cleveland to set aside on January 31, 1886, ten townships of land surrounding Crater Lake.

During the summer, Captain Dutton and William Steel surveyed the lake, providing scientific support for Steel's park idea. The twenty-six-foot boat, the *Cleetwood*, allowed them to conduct

Llao Rock at sunrise. This massive lava flow rests in a crater formed a few hundred years before Mazama's eruption. Note the bed of light pumice under the lava flow. A veneer of pumiceous ash and crystals blankets the top of this glassy dacite dome. Spectacular views of Llao Rock are obtained from the summer boat tours on Crater Lake.

LLOYD SMITH

a thorough examination. Topographer Mark B. Kerr worked on a map of the lake and of the surrounding country. After 168 soundings, they determined the maximum depth to be 1,996 feet. Dutton declared it to be the deepest in the country.

The absence of fish had been noticed during Steel's three weeks on the lake. In August of 1888, Steel, en route to Crater Lake, collected six hundred fingerling trout and carried them forty-nine miles to the lake. Thirty-seven survived the trip. By 1901, some had reached a length of two and a half feet.

Steel wrote numerous magazine and newspaper articles during the next ten years. He sent out a thousand circular letters at his own expense

LARRY SMITH

One of the popular attractions of the boat tours is the "Old Man of the Lake." It was first noted in 1929, but probably was floating around long before that. The Old Man is a hemlock log that was carried into the lake possibly by an avalanche. Rocks, once caught in the roots, caused the log to float vertically in the water. It is seen at random places on the lake as it is driven by wind and water currents.

A winter panorama accessible via the south road, which is kept open all year to Rim Village.

to nearly all the large daily newspapers in the country, asking for support. He also wrote to every newspaper editor and postmaster in Oregon urging them to circulate petitions. When these efforts produced little support, he wrote a 112-page book entitled *The Mountains of Oregon*, which was mailed to the President, his cabinet, and Congress. Steel kept up a virtual blizzard of letter writing for the next sixteen years.

During this period, a legislative bill calling for either a state or national park around Crater Lake was introduced every year in Congress. But lumbermen, sheep ranchers, and land speculators successfully lobbied against each bill. During these disappointing years, Steel continued to spread the fame of Crater Lake by inviting the rich and influential to join him on excursions there.

The Mazamas, a mountain-climbing club founded by Steel, met at Crater Lake during the summer of 1896, two years after the club's charter signing on the summit of eleven thousand-foot Mount Hood. It occurred to them that the ancestral mountain of Crater Lake lacked a name.

Mazama, a South American word for mountain goat, was proposed. Fay Fuller, the first woman to climb Mount Rainier, formally christened the mountain by breaking a bottle of water from the lake against a rock on the rim.

Scientific studies during the 1890s solved many geological mysteries of Crater Lake, further emphasizing the importance of preserving it. A series of compromises, including allowing mining inside the park, and civilian rather than army control, made the national park bill more acceptable to its critics. Steel's petitions were exhibited in the House of Representatives by the bill's sponsor, Thomas H. Tongue. Even with this additional support, the Speaker of the House still refused to bring the legislation to the floor for a house vote.

Steel, labeled a crackpot and a pest, continued to fight the exploiters with zeal and cheerfulness. "I was licked so often, I got so I liked it," he once said. But in 1902, Steel spoke with several personal friends of Theodore Roosevelt, asking them to urge the President to talk to the Speaker

of the House. The tactic worked, for the Congress finally passed the legislation. On May 22, 1902, the President signed the bill which today makes Crater Lake the fifth oldest national park. Steel's dream had been realized at last. The newspapers of Oregon congratulated him on the completion of his life's work, but Steel soon realized that his work was just beginning.

The first money appropriation by Congress for the park was less than a thousand dollars. By the time the park was ten years old, Steel had convinced a reluctant Congress to appropriate over a hundred thousand dollars for improvements. Due to Steel's efforts, the Rim Drive was completed in 1918. Steel was also instrumental in establishing the Crater Lake Lodge Company, a concessionaire operation which opened in 1915.

In recognition of his success, Steel was appointed the park's second superintendent. Speaking before a national parks conference, he summed up his feelings: "All the money I have is in the park, and if I had more, it would go there, too. This is my life's work."

Crater Lake Lodge first opened in 1915. The National Park Service plans to refurbish and reopen the old lodge by the mid 1990s.

Crater Lake in winter. Wizard Island punctuates the lake's blue surface. Mount Scott lies beyond the caldera rim.   NPS PHOTO

To Steel and his supporters, the success of a park was measured by how good the roads were and how many visitors took advantage of such roads. Steel, though active in preservation work, didn't necessarily share the conservation ethic so eloquently established at Yosemite by John Muir, who was interested in preserving the splendor of the solitude. Steel often asked, "What good is scenery if you can't enjoy it fully?" He desired the preservation of Crater Lake so multitudes of visitors, all rubbing shoulders, could stand on the rim and experience the same thrill that had excited him in 1885.

With the establishment of the National Park Commissioner's Court in 1916, Steel resigned as superintendent and accepted an appointment as park commissioner, a position he held until his death in 1934. As transportation improved over the next twenty years, park visitation increased dramatically. Steel spent much of this period traveling around the country encouraging people to visit Crater Lake National Park.

In 1930, Steel prophetically wrote, ". . . my heart bounds with joy and gladness, for I realize that I have been the cause of opening up this wonderful lake for the pleasure of mankind, millions of whom will come and enjoy it. Unborn generations will profit by its glories. Money knows no charm like this."

Two years prior to his death, while sitting on the rim, Steel remarked to a friend, "I have accomplished that which I set out to do and now I am happy."

SUGGESTED READING

CLARK, ELLA E. *Indian Legends of the Pacific Northwest.* Los Angeles, California: University of California Press, 1958.

CRESSMAN, L. S. *The Sandal and the Cave, The Indians of Oregon.* Portland, Oregon: University of Oregon, Beaver Books, 1960.

HECKERT, ELIZABETH. *The People and the River, The Story of the Upper Rogue Valley Indians.* Ashland, Oregon: 1977.

HOWE, CARROL B. *Ancient Modocs of California and Oregon.* Portland, Oregon: Binford and Mort, 1979.

HOWE, CARROL B. *Ancient Tribes of the Klamath Country.* Portland, Oregon: Binford and Mort, 1968.

PLACE, HOWARD and MARIAN. *The Story of Crater Lake National Park.* Idaho: Caxton Printers, 1974.

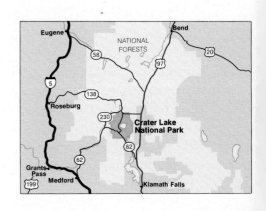

UMPQUA NATIONAL FOREST

Sherwood Butte

230

Rogue River

Boundary Springs

DESERT RIDGE

Devil's Peak

North Entrance Station

Summit Rock

North

0   1   2 Kilometers
0   1   2 Miles

Pacific Crest Trail

Other hiking trail

Ranger station

Picnic area

Campground

Gasoline

138

Bald Crater

Desert Cone

PUMICE DESERT

Timber Crater

WINEMA NATIONAL FOREST

Oasis Butte

Sphagnum Bog

Red Cone

Grouse Hill

Sharp Peaks

Bear Butte

Bear Creek

Scout Hill

Cleetwood Trail

Llao Rock

CLEETWOOD COVE

Rim Drive (Closed in winter)

Wineglass

Devil's Backbone

Rim Drive (Closed in winter)

CRATER LAKE

Maximum lake depth:
589 meters
1932 feet

Skell Head

The Watchman

WIZARD ISLAND

Lake surface elevation:
1882 meters
6176 feet

Cloudcap

Mount Scott
2721 meters

Lightning Spring

Discovery Point

Castle Rock

Pacific Crest Trail

Rim Village Visitor Center
Sinnott Memorial Overlook

Kerr Notch

Cafeteria
Rim Center

Crater Lake Lodge

Phantom Ship

Dutton Cliff

62

Park Headquarters
Information

Sun Notch

Castle Crest Wildflower Trail

Castle Creek

Bybee

Thousand Springs

Watchman Point

Vidae Falls

Sun Creek

Sand Creek

Annie Spring Entrance Station

Annie Spring

Rim Drive (Closed in winter)

Sand Creek

Castle Point

Duwee Falls

Bear Creek

RIVER NAL EST

Mazama

Godfrey Glen Trail
Annie Spring Canyon Trail

Arant Point

Sand Creek

THE PINNACLES

Crater Peak

Quillwort Pond

Union Peak

Maklaks Crater

Huckleberry Mountain

Rocktop Butte

PUMICE FLAT

Scoria Cone

232

Bald Top

Stuart Falls

Goose Nest

WINEMA

47

Crater Lake Today

The National Park Service has entered into an enlightened period of management. Today, the emphasis is on maintaining the ecosystems which support all native species—including man. Studies continue to yield valuable data on the natural systems which created Crater Lake. Such studies will aid the National Park Service in protecting this unique region for the enjoyment of future generations. Thanks to the preservation efforts and foresight of William G. Steel, Crater Lake will gain in importance as a refuge where nature is unchanged by the works of man.

Crater Lake is one of the few wild places left where we can practice the fine art of living in the open. Here, we may forget ourselves for a time and enjoy a surge of healthy outdoor exploration. Here, we may rediscover ourselves and learn that material things don't necessarily constitute our richest possessions. The blue gem of the Cascades moves us deeply when we imagine the infinite power which created this wonderful place called Crater Lake.

DAVID MUENCH

The forces of volcanic mountain-building and the destructive elements of weather have created Crater Lake.

NEW: in pictures—The Continuing Story: Bryce Canyon, Death Valley, Everglades, Grand Canyon, Mount Rainier, Mount St. Helens, Petrified Forest, Sequoia-Kings Canyon, Yellowstone, Yosemite, Zion.
Books in the Story Behind the Scenery series: Acadia, Alcatraz Island, Arches, Biscayne, Blue Ridge Parkway, Bryce Canyon, Canyon de Chelly, Canyonlands, Cape Cod, Capitol Reef, Channel Islands, Civil War Parks, Colonial, Crater Lake, Death Valley, Denali, Devils Tower, Dinosaur, Everglades, Fort Clatsop, Gettysburg, Glacier, Glen Canyon-Lake Powell, Grand Canyon, Grand Canyon-North Rim, Grand Teton, Great Basin, Great Smoky Mountains, Haleakala, Hawaii Volcanoes, Independence, Lake Mead-Hoover Dam, Lassen Volcanic, Lincoln Parks, Mammoth Cave, Mount Rainier, Mount Rushmore, Mount St. Helens, National Park Service, National Seashores, North Cascades, Olympic, Petrified Forest, Redwood, Rocky Mountain, Scotty's Castle, Sequoia-Kings Canyon, Shenandoah, Statue of Liberty, Theodore Roosevelt, Virgin Islands, Yellowstone, Yosemite, Zion.

Published by KC Publications • Box 14883 • Las Vegas, NV 89114

Sunrise through storm fog gives warm glow to Crater Lake
DAVID MUENC

Back cover: Winter transforms the tranquil waters into a sapphire set in a sea of white.
RAY ATKESON

Printed by Dong-A Printing and Publishing, Seoul, Korea
Color Separations by Kedia/Kwangyangsa Co., Ltd.